W9-DHU-547

What you see
is NOT what you do

A Simple Formula for Ballroom Dancing

By Nick and Lena Kosovich

©2012 Big Life Publishing

Published by Big Life Publishing

ISBN 978-1-933649-01-6

By Nick and Lena Kosovich with Jane Melvin
Design and layout by Jane Ackerson

First Edition
Copyright © 2012 Big Life Publishing
Some material Copyright © 2012 Nikoz International (cited within text)
All rights reserved.

For more information, visit us at www.lenique.com.

Dedication

Many people in our lives have influenced, changed,
driven, inspired and shared their love for dance with us;
we feel their spirit and influence every
time we take the floor.

We dedicate this book to the dancers no
longer with us who shared their passion for dance
and inspired us and others before us.
They will not be forgotten - with every step in every dance,
each of those remarkable artists continues to move us all.

And of course, with the most love and
gratitude to our families.

Dance with Passion

Nick + Lena Kosovich

Acknowledgements

Most of all, we thank our teachers, some from the ballroom world and some our other worlds... To our dance teachers old and new, we hope we don't miss anyone, but here goes.

Australasia

Clive & Anne Dorney, Keith & Marita Withers, Bob, Sheryl and Barry Wrightson, Robert Boyd, Peter & Roslyn Smith, Lee & Cheryl Wilton, Peter Todd, Ron Barker, Len & Pamela Humphreys, Charles Froulop, Phillip Logan, Ray & Margaret Reeve, Neville Boyd OAM, Bernie Rielly, Alex & Julie Schembri, Doug & Sue Potter, Doug Newton, Neil & Jenny Rosenfeld, Les & Julie Patchett, Kerry Wilson

Europe

Lubov Urbin-Vasilieva, Alla & Peter Chebotarev, Ludmila & Stanislav Popov, Colin James, Johan & Nadia Eftedal, Michael Stylianos & Lorna Lee, Allan & Hazel Fletcher, Walter Laird, Nina Hunt, Benny Tolmeyer, Bill & Bobbie Irvine MBE, Sonny Binnick, Hans Laxholm, Bob Burgess, Anthony Hurley, Richard & Janet Gleave, Andrew Sinkinson, Charlotte Jorgenson, Luca & Lorraine Baricci, Kenny & Marion Welsh, Ruud Vermeij, Peter Townsend, The 'Lorraine', Joe & Katia Vanone, Pamela McGill, Dorothy Charlton, Allan Tornsberg, June McMurdoe, Katerina Arzenton, John Delroy

USA

Taliat & Marina Tarsinov, John Nyemchek, Rufus Dustin, Brian & Kristi McDonald, John Kimmins, Pete Taylor, Ken & Sheila Sloan, Ron Montez, Liz Curtis, Peter Di Falco, L V Amstel, Joe Jenkins, Beverly Donahue, John Ford & Margueruite Hanlon, Jim Donaghay & Judi Hatton , Maria Torres, John Festa, Frankie Manning, Martin Lamb, Paul Holmes, Wendy Johnson, Lisa Barishnikov, Terry Leone

Table of Contents

Foreward

"Someone Ought To Write a Book About That!"

US Smooth Champions Nick and Lena Kosovich don't talk much about how this book came to life – why, after a lifetime of dancing they finally decided to put it down on paper. A tiny event became the catalyst. The way it happened speaks volumes about Nick and Lena and what resulted in this book.

They were teaching a master class, talking about their philosophy of the dance and of ways to learn the basics of the ballroom. They talked about why they thought the way they thought and teach the way they teach.

And they remember that on that particular day they said, "and someone should write a book about that." One of the students in the class mouthed, "you should."

Well, I was that student.

After the class I went over to say thank you and said, "This was great – you really should write that book because I won't be able to remember everything and I wish I'd been taking notes."

And that was that. And here we are. Although I'm sure they've had thousands of requests to do it before they ever met me, for some reason, on that day, in that place, it all began. It was one of those strange things. Perhaps it was a coincidence or just that I was a naïve new-to-the-ballroom student and didn't know any better way to learn than to take notes and study them. I didn't know at the time but I think now it really was meant to be, since when Nick said it, in a room full of people, he happened to be looking right at me.

There were about 40 people in that masters' workshop. We were all thrilled at the chance to experience a class with these two champion dancers: ABC's "Dancing With the Stars" had just begun and Nick and Lena were fresh from appearances on the show.

Despite being brand new to the ballroom at the time and having no idea what a lot of it really meant, I knew what I was hearing was important. Although at the time I only knew them by reputation, somehow I sensed that if he said "Ok" that meant "let's make it happen."

In the class, I'd heard some pretty intriguing ideas, but most of it went right over my head. I was beginning my own love affair with the sport, and I had the chance to hear from some pretty great teachers thanks to the studio where I danced. So I invested heavily, racing ahead in my own study of ballroom dancing so I could learn enough to ask the right questions while we got Nick and Lena's ideas down on paper. I've worked hard to understand some of the lessons in this book by trying to experience them through my own lessons and practice. I went to their classes over and over and listened to their ideas again and again.

Some days I feel I'm actually on the verge of physically experiencing what they are teaching… and some days I just know I need a lot more lessons and more practice than the years left in my hips will allow. But I am learning, thanks to the chance I've had to go back and read it again, and practice it, and try new things and practice it again. In the course of this project I've attempted to help Nick and Lena articulate their ideas in a way that works for a beginning dancer as well as someone who's spent decades in the ballroom.

From my own experience as a student while this has been happening, I know that what Nick and Lena teach has great value to any level dancer. I was right that day - that class was jam-packed with information you'll find in this book. Over the many years spent working on this, I've learned more and more but I still find new value every time I think through the concepts in these chapters.

It also says a lot about Nick and Lena that they were willing to filter their ideas through the lens of a very new student. What an incredible sport it is, one where the newest people can get a taste of the very things the world champions are working on and have the chance to come back to it time after time as their mastery progresses.

This project was a chance to combine something I do (articulate and communicate ideas that help people live their big lives) with an activity and art form I've come to love. This is most definitely an expression of Nick and Lena's concepts and philosophy. But I hope I have helped them express these powerful ideas. A little music for their dance.... or lyrics for their song....

But there is something else. It was at that first moment during the master class where I sensed the most unique thing about Nick and Lena. Yes, they are professional dance champions and entrepreneurs and designers and artists. They are as competitive as people come and as dedicated as athletes can be. But through the process of bringing this book to life I have been amazed at something I have now come to understand as the refreshing and inspiring sense of possibility I felt in those first moments.

Nick and Lena create things from only a hint of an idea, a breath of a thought, a slice of music, a swatch of fabric, a piece of fur or a rhinestone that sparkles a particular way in the light. They pounce on the smallest bit of inspiration and turn it into something big. It's how they think. It's how they dance. And it's how they live.

I have laughed through the process of putting this book together with them. They could not be more different – his Australian optimism, her deep Russian soul... they create energy just by being in a room together. They are an unexpected combination. They show how a true partnership can manifest in something delightful and surprising, taking the gifts of each and creating something truly magnificent together. Strong on their own. Unstoppable together.

As we worked on this book, I came to respect something else very special about Nick and Lena and their ballroom community: there is a tremendous sense of gratitude that drives a responsibility they take very seriously.

They are actively and passionately appreciative of all the coaches and teachers in their lives. They love to teach and constantly evolve their teaching. They never ever forget the many people who helped them become the dancers they are.

Nick lights up when he talks about some of the ballroom greats he has known, of listening to them debate late into the night the finer points of the way you move your body weight on a tiny piece of a particular step.

Lena often jumps up from her chair and demonstrates techniques she picked up from treasured coaches, translating words from many languages into her own

iv

movement. Walking down the street, she will suddenly execute a beautiful twinkle with a lamp post (I've seen her do it!). There's a smile on her face, and a light in her eyes as she demonstrates what she means when she tells you to find the clarity in the movement.

They are among the best: their skills, their dedication, their pursuit of their craft. I have signed up for coaching with Lena when we are lucky enough to have her in our studio and heard her say, "what size knives do I need to get out for this lesson?" I have seen her adjust a dancer's arm an almost imperceptible amount and completely change the outcome of the movement. I have watched Nick stride across the ballroom floor in what I swear were three steps and watched him pause, almost hanging in the air, as the music fills the room. His eyes light up when he hears a "cool new arrangement of a song" or when he senses he is on the verge of a new idea. They both find ways to connect what each student is doing to the basic concepts of teaching they share in this book.

They can't just show up – they have to be full in.

When I went to that master class at that wonderful Arthur Murray studio, I'd been dancing for all of three months. I'd seen Nick and Lena on TV and I'd seen them perform in a professional show the night before at a charity event.

I looked around the room and I watched the other 40 people in that workshop. Some had danced for years and some, like me, were brand new. Each person was completely immersed. There was truly something for everyone in that class. The teachers were taking notes at a furious pace, the gifted amateurs were trying the exercises, and my head felt like it would explode trying to remember it all.

I knew this was something that had to be captured so it could be shared. It's taken a while – after all, we've all been busy dancing – but here it is, at long last.

My passion is about discovering and living your big life. My relatively new hobby of ballroom dancing has helped me find and add sparkle to my own, and I know when I see others who are living theirs. Ballroom dancing – as a profession, as an art form, as a craft to be perfected, as a passion and as a life pursuit for Nick and Lena – is how they are living theirs.

My calling is to help people find and express their big lives. I've been lucky to help get down on paper what Nick and Lena think about and teach every day. I hope in this book you read not only an instruction manual about dancing, but also feel their contagious sense of possibility. Nick and Lena have it in abundance and sprinkle it like fairy dust wherever they go. They are incredible dancers and they are pretty special human beings.

We should all live with the active gratitude they have for their teachers and we should all find ways to share what we absorb from our big lives with others.

Jane Melvin
March, 2012

Chapter One:
A Product of Partnership

This book is a labor of love. We've spent so much of our lives on the ballroom floor, and we have spent the best of those competitive years with each other. We are privileged to be able to dance for a living, and inspired now to share our love of dance with other people in so many ways. Like all professional artists, we worked hard to achieve what we have, but we also know in our hearts we're still the dreamers who took to the floor that very first time, eager to start, a little intimidated and very, very hungry to learn.

Learning to dance as children, we simply plunged in. Because we were children, we were fearless – we saw no boundaries and we didn't impose restrictions on ourselves. We never knew where it would take us, but the dreams it inspired and the blessings we have achieved through our lives in the ballroom have been incredible. Coming from opposite sides of the planet and ending up in a partnership that yielded so much has been a truly amazing ride. Finding each other over a decade ago, joining our two separate paths… maybe it was destiny… maybe chance… or maybe just plain good luck.

Our passion for dance as a profession has allowed us to travel around the world doing ballroom performances. We design one-of-a-kind costumes for dancers who come to us with their ideas and entrust us with expressing their deepest creative selves. The company we've created – LeNique – is yet another way to connect to the world of ballroom and gives us the chance to help our clients feel more confident as they pursue their own love of dance.

What we love the most is sharing our experience, sharing some of what we have learned and some of the ideas we've developed over the years that are at the root of how we became champion dancers. Although we retired from professional competition, we still try to learn, to grow and to improve. We've observed and practiced and tried things that failed. All of these experiences are the foundation for the ideas we share here.

There are two sides of teaching. The obvious is that of the teacher. But we are also perpetual students and we learn every time we teach. This is yet another form of partnership, and one that is critical to the ever-evolving art of the ballroom. The relationship of teacher and student comes naturally to us now because the process of learning is the very essence of ballroom dancing: partnership, trust and mutual desire to achieve.

When we were competing, this focus was turned inward, to our relationship with each other and how it manifested on the dance floor. Our partnership with our own teachers focused on making us better dancers. Now, we turn that more outward – the partnership that comes from teaching and learning is something everyone who goes to a class or takes a lesson can embrace. We are touched by our students, by people we see changing and transforming their lives, people who are hungry to learn and dying to dance.

We see people who have gone out dancing every Thursday for 35 years, people who dance at weddings – the ones

2

who look like they have danced together for a lifetime - people who come in for a little exercise and leave feeling rejuvenated and happy. We see people in their 80's who are just stepping onto the ballroom floor for the first time and people going through major life transitions. We see teachers who teach others to dance and professionals who are working harder than they ever imagined, improving their already world-class dancing. Every one of them adds to our experience and shapes our coaching repertoire. They challenge and confirm our ideas and help us find new ways to bring more relevance to our lessons.

Whenever we teach, people ask us if we've ever written it down. They want something they can take with them to study and think about the ideas that we discuss in our workshops and lessons and coaching sessions.

It's probably hard for any teacher to ever "write it all down" because the best teachers are always learning. Everything we do teaches us something… whether it is a new way to talk about a concept, a new exercise that seems to connect with a student, or seeing our professional couples grow and improve and remembering how we helped them. Often we feel like we are channeling the spirits of our own teachers and coaches, so many of whom have shaped our dancing; we are passionate about passing along our experience to others. That is the gift of this community of the ballroom… the appreciation of our heritage and the responsibility we have to help continue the dance.

Writing down the collection of concepts that are ever evolving is a challenging task. We feel like we could write volumes (and we will – this is just the first of many, we hope!). We've spent hours and days and weeks getting coached by the best in the world and coaching other dancers. No matter how advanced the coach or how sophisticated the teaching techniques, there are some basic principles we've tested around the world and we've found to be relevant to dancers at any level, from a beginner to a teacher to a professional competitor. We've worked with thousands of dancers around the world but we've found that we come back to the same basic concepts in all our work. The essence of our teaching is the same – our concepts are a long-evolved hybrid of expertise, coaching and the school of hard knocks.

So the time finally came to write it down. So many people had asked for "notes" or if there was further material available after a workshop. It just seemed right that we would do this together – while we both can teach workshops on dance and we can both lead and we can both follow, we have experienced the very special phenomenon in life that you find when individually you are good but together you are exponentially better. That formula worked for us when we competed together, it works for us as we run our business, and we thought it was the only way to go when we decided to take on this project.

During the development of this book, we were privileged to have some terrific ballroom experts review it and give us their input. Not everyone agreed with our approach and not everyone had heard the ideas described this way. For us, that is yet another rich piece of the ballroom experience - many people have many different points of view about this art form and many of us don't agree. Many people have and should write books about the technique and physical science of dance. We care a great deal about that, but we have a different point of view. This is not a book about steps. It is a book about dancing, about feeling the music and translating it into movement.

4

Many people questioned whether it should even be a book. As one of our favorite professional dancers said, "Well this is why you can't really learn to dance from a book - it's just not about words!" We agree. You can't really learn to dance from a book - but we do think you can find new ways to think about what you do and new ways to think about the challenge of dancing.

We hope you will use this book as a reference piece, a reminder, and perhaps a kind of inspiration. Your experience on the floor and with your own great teachers cannot ever be replaced. But we hope our perspective will help your dancing, and help the way you think about your dancing.

Dancing is a lifetime journey and so is partnership. We expect in ten years we will want to rewrite this book since we are continuing to learn about dancing and how to teach it and we hope by then there will be more books in our collection. For now, we hope this helps give you a resource you haven't had before. As you read this book, please remember that after all the theory and exercise and practice, the most important ingredient in great dancing is that you take your heart onto the dance floor.

Put everything you have in it. And (Lena reminds us) practice, practice, practice.

Chapter Two:
What You See Is Not What You Do

Often when we teach a master class we begin by saying that most of the significant books about ballroom dancing have been written by people who watched the best dancers in the world and wrote about what they saw. But what no one explains is that what someone sees when he or she watches and what someone does when he or she dances are often so different that it can really surprise you.

Our approach is to focus on what the dancer must DO to achieve what others see. It's not just a matter of following step patterns. It's about understanding each component of every action that goes into movement and then making each part of that action appropriate for the dance you are doing.

Although we learned to dance in different hemispheres with very different approaches, we were learning the same partner dances to the same strict tempo music with ambitions of competing at the highest possible levels. When we eventually got together we realized our combined knowledge was a powerful tool. Lena focused – and still does – more on the action you are attempting, doing it over and over and over again to achieve clarity in each and every movement. Nick focused more on the components of the action – what made a particular turn, for example, feel different from one dance than the same turn does in another, how to incorporate those differences you feel from the music into physical expression.

Despite these different emphases, the more we watched each other teach, the more we saw that our destination was the same. We both put great value in the character and feel of each dance. We both worked hard to understand the physical dynamics of leading and following.

We first developed our approaches separately, and then refined it together. The more we taught, the more we observed that one thing is true about every student we've ever had: there comes a point when they realize "it's not the way it looks."

This "aha" moment is a physical sensation.

It could be a moment in a waltz when the dancer realizes he or she must really drag – and we mean push hard - their feet across the floor, as if they were being pulled down into it, and they realize they actually cover more distance. They finally experience the ultimate in counter-intuition and paradox…. How could pushing that hard, down in to the floor, make you move so far, feel so light and appear to be skimming the surface? How is it that you have to push down to go up?

This "aha" could be a moment when the person stretches to the point where he or she feels a little silly but sees in the mirror that she actually looks beautiful in that movement. It could be the instant you see that a moment of stillness can add tremendous emphasis to the next moment of movement.

We hope through sharing our approach we can accelerate that "aha" moment for you. Once you feel it, you can begin to apply the thinking across every movement in every dance. We've come up with a framework for it and we hope it will help you experience these important lessons – and move from understanding it in theory to being able to do it in practice.

Our "formula" for the ballroom is based not on what you see, but rather on what you *do*.

While all dances include the same *actions*, it takes different *effort* and a different sense of *character* to create them in a way that is suitable and appropriate for the character of each dance. Because you are dancing with the partner, it is critical that you agree to and move in a common *direction*, and it's essential that you use the *natural* forces of the ballroom – music, and the connection to you partner - to accomplish the movement.

Each piece of it is important and no question about it, there is a lot to remember. Take it in small pieces or read through it in longer spurts. To try to help you do that, we've divided this into five different chunks and within each chunk there are several key concepts for you to study and then practice. We've laid it out in the order we think makes sense – what you should be thinking about when you step onto the floor through to what you should be working on to add artistry and interest to your dancing.

However you decide to tackle these lessons, try to take the words we've written and translate them into a physical practice. This is the point where Lena would say, "Nick, stop talking about it and just do it - you can't explain it with more words. You just have to feel it!"

8

In the process of writing this book, we shared our ideas and approaches with many experts from the ballroom word. Not everyone agreed with what we said. Some had not thought about things this way and many had their own ways of teaching, as well as different priorities about what to teach when, and about what causes a certain result. It's important to remember that ballroom dancing is an art. As a result, it feels very subjective sometimes and artists have many different points of view.

Our perspective is based on one single foundation idea: that you can experience a physical sensation of movement in many different ways but it is the *action* and the *effort* and the movement that make up the dance. Starting with an end goal of clarity of movement, we break the movement down into pieces. We hope our descriptions, ideas, metaphors and exercises will help you understand this basic idea.

We know, having gone through this process, why there aren't many books about ballroom dancing – it's quite challenging to translate movement into words. We encourage you to try to feel in your body what we mean in our words. As we worked on this book we were often struck by how hard it is to explain a physical concept through a set of words on the page – it would be so much easier to just demonstrate it for you. We encourage you to keep taking lessons, to attend workshops (particularly when we come to town to teach!) so that you can use this book as a reference point and always concentrate on what it feels like when you actually practice what we say.

Imagine that Nick is standing next to you pushing you to separate the actions in your movement.

Imagine Lena asks you to do it again. And again. Until you achieve clarity in the movement.

Chapter Three:
Our "Simple" Formula

Our simple formula combines decades of dance theory, stretching from the concepts of Laban to the notion of choreology to the philosophies of many coaches, but it's how we put it together that makes it our own teaching philosophy. We use the lens of our own experience and we ground it in the physical sense of what you must *DO* to achieve your goals.

We like to explain it this way: it's much less about the steps you take than how you take the steps.

Most dancers – from a beginner to an expert – work on the same challenges. While you may be new to the ballroom, your desire to improve your dance frame is the same as a veteran professional who may be competing at the highest levels. Most dancers are – and should – be working on the same basic ideas. We've isolated these areas and then divided them into pieces so you can tackle them a piece at a time.

Our approach includes five components. We find these to be the areas we concentrate on in our teaching, coaching and judging. These are the areas where progress and mastery separates good dancers from great dancers. For each of the five major areas, there is one main idea, but unlimited opportunity to improve and change how you dance. Each main idea is broken into pieces.

We begin with the physical fundamentals, those things that you do to create a strong foundation for great partnership and great individual dancing. We then layer on artistry and what each unique dancer decides will be the character and style of his or her dancing. Finally, we work on how to get the most out of each action in the movement.

Our formula is simple and easy to remember. How do you become a better ballroom dancer? DANCE.

Each stage includes many concepts you can study, learn and practice. Each part is related to the others. Each part on its own will drive you to a more satisfying level of dancing. Each contains a very specific set of concepts to learn and then put into physical practice.

Together, the pieces combine into a philosophy that will help you...DANCE.

As you consider this approach as a way to improve your dancing, here are a couple of tips to help you get the most out of your investment.

Be Clear About What You Are Trying to Learn

Like any project you take on, you need to have a clear idea of what you want to learn, and what you want the outcome to be.

11

Break It Into Pieces

Effective learning comes from taking it a piece at a time. We encourage you to read through the entire approach first and understand it intellectually, then break up the pieces and try to practice things one piece at a time.

Don't be frustrated when you can't do these things the first time or the hundredth time. Keep going.

Don't be fooled to think ah, now I have the book so it will be easier. It won't. It might even make it feel overwhelming. However, we will give you a vocabulary of learning that will help you and we will cover all the areas you need to become a dramatically better dancer, no matter where you are starting. A lot of the concepts are still things that we work on when we practice. Remember... a significant part of the power of dance is that you can always get better. Also remember that we've spent a combined eight decades building our experience and trying to fit it into a book. It will definitely take more than reading it once!

Here are all the topics we cover in this book:

D DIRECTION	A ACTIONS	N NATURE	C CHARACTER	E EFFORT
Leading	Bending	Timing	Waltz	Weight
Following	Traveling	Tempo	Tango	Energy
Individual Roles	Twisting	Breath	Foxtrot	Space
Structure	Turning	Connection	V. Waltz	Time
Tension	Contracting		Quickstep	
Tone	Stretching		Rumba	
Torque	Balancing		Cha Cha	
			Swing	
			Jive	
			Balero	
			Mambo	

12 © 2011 Big Life Publishing

All Learning is Comparative and Contextual

We've built a lot of comparisons into this book. We compare dances with each other. We provide perspectives and tips for the leader and the follower. We provide alternative viewpoints on the character of each of the dances we discuss. For example, the concept of **effort** is explained through a simple and comparative method. We find it much easier to understand how things differ if you can compare one dance with another.

We often define each of the basic elements by two opposite concepts or feelings. Each dance is one or the other. By thinking about the characteristics of the dances in different ways, you might be surprised at how some dances are similar and some that you think might be similar are actually really different. You will note that we don't go into great detail on each dance – that will come in the next book!

Try To Keep It Simple

Dancing – like most art forms – is incredibly complex and intricate. As learners and teachers we have to force ourselves to simplify, organize and prioritize. Once you've done that it's much easier to figure out what you are actually practicing or changing. We explain the concepts here in simple and visual language and we provide you with a variety of exercises that will help you isolate and develop action and movement to help your dancing.

Don't Go It Alone

Partnership is the foundation of the ballroom. People who dance love to talk about it so don't think you are out there alone. We encourage you to start small, to think about the big picture but then break it down. Talk about it with your partner, your teacher and your dancing friends. Debate it. Try it. Practice it. Analyze it. Have fun with it. Download video demonstrations and lessons. Ask someone to video tape your next performance. Watch it. Review it with your teacher or your partners. See if you can see examples of what we're talking about in the book. Watch the professionals dance. At the next exhibition or competition, ask your teacher to point out a dancer who does a particularly good job in an area you are working on.

And then try it again.

Practice Makes Perfect

The old cliché is right on. You can never ever practice enough. ("Trust me on this one," says Nick, "I'm married to a Russian dancer who started this at seven years old!") The concepts we explain here are the secret to our dancing and serve as the foundation of all our teaching and coaching. We encourage you to put these concepts to work in your dancing right away. Strike the right balance in your learning. The more experienced you are the more challenging the changes you make. Small adjustments take lots of time and practice. Don't get frustrated. Keep trying.

Don't overcomplicate. Think carefully and work on specific changes, one at a time.

The concepts are simple but their power is limitless.

So now, let's break it into pieces and start at the beginning.

Chapter Four:
Set the Direction

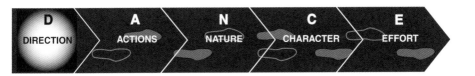

D	A	N	C	E
DIRECTION	ACTIONS	NATURE	CHARACTER	EFFORT

There are a few special characteristics about ballroom dancing that make it distinct from other forms of dance. The most significant is that ballroom dancing is partner dancing. Your partner is there for a reason. Having a partner changes the way you channel your energy. It changes the way you move. It changes the way you find balance. It also means that the partnership is made up of three components: you, me and us.

Yes, you have to dance for yourself, but your energy is integrally linked to your partner's. Truly mastering great fundamentals of dancing ballroom depends on taking maximum advantage of the partnership, both in how you contribute to it and how you benefit from it. It's making the most of "the you, the me and the us."

At the beginning, you have very different roles, but the longer you dance, and the longer you dance together, you'll realize that you are ultimately moving as one, and the most important way to make a great partnership is to establish a strong foundation, individually and as a couple, early on. So, first rule of ballroom dancing. Learn your part. Then learn your partnership.

Leading and Following

A great way to start is to be clear about your role as a leader or a follower. Understand what you need to contribute in your role, and then set yourself up for success by working hard to achieve a great dance frame before you even take a step. This is the best possible contribution to the partnership because it is what allows leading and following to take place.

Then you can begin. Simple. How?

One person leads.

One person follows.

Think of leading and following as a conversation. While each person has a different job, leading and following requires a constant exchange of non-verbal signals and information. Remember that it is a two-way conversation. If there isn't a follower, whom do you lead? At the beginning the roles are clear but as dancers become more advanced, you might begin to notice that sometimes in the middle of things, these roles switch and switch back in the blink of an eye. For the most part, though, it's pretty simple and most dancers won't need to worry much about that.

One of our pet peeves is the notion that the leader is the frame and follower is the picture – somehow this implies that they can exist without each other. We believe the two parts are completely equal and important.

Those are the two equal roles – what you do in each role is pretty clear as well:

- Whoever is leading is providing positive clear direction and timing.
- Whoever is following is responsible for moving their own body and reacting to the leader's direction and timing.

The more complex part is that each partner also has to contribute individually. We like to think of your individual responsibilities as follows. Each dancer must:

- Clearly set individual direction – then join it with the partner
- Be responsible for 100% of his or her own movement
- Maintain proper posture and dance frame
- Know how to either create energy or hold energy within his or her own connection and frame
- Contribute the appropriate weight and energy to create an active connection
- Actively have a "sense of feel" for the other partner's body weight and then respond to their weight and energy.

When leading and following is at its best, each partner finds their physical center. Each partner is able to balance, take the clear steps that serve as the foundation of their style and expression, and feel strong and firm in their place with each other.

You bring these responsibilities to life through your whole body. We call the readiness and physical manifestation of these individual responsibilities your "dance frame" – it is the immediate physical space you own and operate when you are out on the floor. Think of your dance frame as part of your overall "structure" – a structure that includes your frame, your hold, and all the connection points with your partner.

Be warned that you will probably work on your frame throughout your life as a dancer and that once you improve one thing there will always be a way to work on something else. A dance frame is a journey. Although we would like it to be a destination, it is a journey that with a little understanding you can be well prepared for before you begin.

Developing Your Frame

A great frame allows you to "dance yourself." You must keep your frame strong and sure so that if you are leading you can give clear direction and if you are following you can be led. Done right, you will feel strong in your frame with a great sense of balance and the ability to do the moves with style, speed and strength. Done wrong, you might pull on your partner in an unhelpful way; you might end up muscling your way though a step instead of truly dancing it. A great frame is as much about the way it feels to your partner as it appears in your posture and poise. Without a great frame, the leader can feel like he is trying to drive a truck or direct Jell-o and the follower can feel a total lack of direction, resulting in confusion and frustration. With a great frame, a follower can dance steps she didn't know she knew, simply because she is in the correct position and can accept the direction as the leader supplies it.

The secret to your frame is to understand and apply **tension, tone and torque**. Knowing the difference between these concepts will help you put them to work

18

in the appropriate manner. We guarantee this will make a huge difference in your leading and following skills. Understanding these ideas will give your body and muscles a vocabulary so you can isolate what you want them to do. First and foremost, you are working to inject tone into your dancing body. Tone is an extremely physical concept. In dance it is not the same as it is in the gym. Often, people describe an in-shape, strong athlete as having great "muscle tone." In dance, tone is more of an active state.

Tone is a very difficult concept to describe in words. It's a sensation, a physical feeling and it would be a lot easier to understand it if you could strip away your skin and see what the muscles do... and while we know progress sometimes takes pain, we don't mean that kind of pain!

The way to understand what tone is is to compare it to what it isn't, and to understand the sensations it takes to create tone within your body.

Hold that thought and let's try to put it in a context by comparing it to what it isn't.

Tension is the engagement of an isolated muscle or muscle group with no countering force. It's isometric, focused and concentrated. The power and energy it creates flows in one direction. Lift something heavy. Most people tense their muscles to do that.

Torque is two muscles or muscle groups working against each other. It is forceful, powerful and aggressive, and it feels like you are working your muscles really hard, sort of like a screwdriver working to tighten the last bit of a screw into concrete. The energy that flows from it feels very directed into one spot, but you can feel the energy moving against something else.

Imagine a spectrum where tension lies at one end and torque lies at the other.

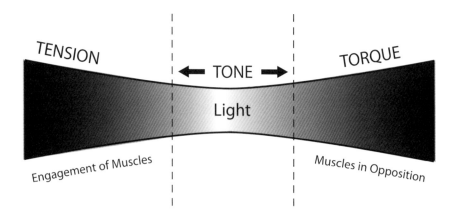

Tone lies at the midpoint between tension and torque. It is the engagement of a group of muscles in balanced opposition to each other. It is a state of balanced effort that allows you to control your energy, give or receive physical signals from your partner and move, all at the same time. It feels engaged, calm, and firm.

Think of tone as a state in which you counterbalance tension and incorporate gentle torque. Feel strong, quiet and ready to begin.

We use all three of these concepts in dancing. We constantly use tone and tension to varying degrees in different parts of our bodies. We gain power from using them - tone and tension drives the effort that creates action.

Here are some exercises that should help you understand – and more importantly, feel – these concepts in your body. Remember, think of tension as the engagement of a single

20

muscle. You stretch and engage the muscle. Flex your bicep. Engage your quad. These are relatively easy to command and easy to do because they are simple things – you don't even really have to think about it.

Now, stand straight up with your arms extended out to your sides. Rotate your body to the left and then to the right. Don't put any particular effort into your arms except to hold them out straight, parallel to the floor. Let them relax except keep them parallel to the floor. When turning your body quickly, you feel your arms swing – if you do it fast enough, they will go past the point of the rotation of your body.

Now, decide that you want to stop your arms from moving past the point where your torso stops rotating. This is tension. **Tension** is the engagement of the muscle and it will allow you to stop your arms, and stop your rotation. You no longer feel like you are swinging your arms – you are beginning to control the movement.

Tension is what makes you stop movement. It feels stiff. Tension is powerful. Tension is energetic. But consider it through the lens of dance: tension is not tone. Remember, tone is what happens when you use *groups* of muscles in combination instead of individual muscles. You are not neutralizing one with the other, but you are creating exponential energy control. In an odd way it's like the idea of "you, me and us." Two groups of muscles, coordinated in a common pursuit, are much more effective as the sum of the parts.

Groups of muscles in your arms, legs, torso, back and chest serve as a kind of central nervous system for your connection to your partner and allow you to do many things at once – rotate, travel, twist, bend and stretch. Working

21

muscle groups together and against each other creates tone. The best dancers in the world have worked to be able to consistently keep their bodies in an active state of tone while they are whirling around the floor.

Tone contributes your portion of the shared energy you feel in your partner's frame. It is necessary for both the leader and the follower.

The ability to consistently achieve tone is a wonderful asset. While it is extremely difficult to master, you should be optimistic about the ability to eventually do so because it is most definitely a learned skill. While some people appear to be able to achieve tone unconsciously, or naturally, trust us... they had to learn how to do it at some point. It requires focus and good physical discipline.

Some late-comers to the ballroom tell us the older you are when you try to learn it the harder it can be since there is so much "old muscle memory" that creates regular daily movement without using tone. Once you achieve this physical asset of actively creating tone in your body, you will be able to create your own strong and powerful dance frame. The good news is you can practice and retrain your muscles.

Here are some more exercises to try that might help you experience the difference between these three things.

Think about going to the gym to lift weights. Imagine doing a basic bicep curl. Hold the weight, bend your elbow and lift your forearm toward your shoulders. Feel how you are isolating a specific group of muscles in the arm. You're not really working anything else in the arm.

22

Can you feel tension in your muscles?

Now, do a bicep curl while still holding the weight but now twist your arm as you lift. That twist is the torque. As you twist you are creating tone through that twist (or torque). You can feel the effort throughout your whole arm, not just your biceps. Do this a couple of time, even with an imaginary weight. Concentrate on the difference you feel in your arm by lifting the weight first without the twist and then with the twist. You should be able to isolate the difference between tension and torque and you should be able to feel tone as you complete the lift.

Now you can do it in a way that relates directly to your dancing. Go back to the exercise you were doing earlier, where you extended your arms out from your side and rotated our body.

- First, relax your arms and let them hang by your sides.
- Lift them up slowly, stretching outward, engaging your lat muscles in your back as if you are carrying something heavy and your shoulders stay down.   Your arms are active from your back through your fingertips.
- Rotate your entire arm, from your shoulder, toward the ceiling, palms up, so your elbows are facing down.
- Now rotate your elbows only, forward so they are facing towards the ceiling, keeping your shoulders seated down towards the lat muscles in your back.
- Then, slightly twist your wrists back up in the opposing direction so that your palms are facing upwards and in front of you.

If you do it right you'll be engaging each muscle group (that's the *tone*) and twisting them against each other.

(That's the *torque*.) Find the balance point in the middle where you feel engaged, controlled and firm in your muscles.

When you do the rotation exercise, you should feel a tremendous sensation of control over your body. It's not just stop and start – instead, you are controlling your movement in a strong and powerful way. You have achieved tone (by torquing the different groups of muscles in your arms, torso, chest ad back against each other). Now you are in frame. You are commanding your energy. It will feel stiff at first but you will learn to control it while you are moving.

Here's another way you can think about it with a more visual exercise. Think of an airplane and how it flies. Now think of a seagull and how it flies. Both can move from one point to another. An airplane generally does move from one point to another. Its purpose is functional and it can do what we ask of it. A seagull, however, may be fishing or moving or flying or simply playing.

You can sit on a beach for hours and watch it in is graceful flight, up and down and around. Put a soundtrack to those movements in your mind. What does it sound like? It's likely the soundtrack of the airplane is one droning sound. The soundtrack for the art of flight? A beautiful Beethoven symphony? The airplane is like tension – the engagement of one muscle for one purpose, stiff and strong but not creating a feeling of balance or an active state of readiness or motion. The seagull flies in a way that seems more like tone and torque. It can move artfully in any direction with grace.

When you set up your frame you begin to feel the tone. A great dance frame means you are creating tone throughout your entire body - from the position of your fingertips and the tone in your arms through your back and core and legs and feet.

Dance Your Whole Body

Often, when we are coaching beginning dancers, our clearest advice to them might be to "dance your whole body." They might be so busy learning patterns that they might not know what that means. Using the concepts we've outlined above will help move beyond simple step patterns.

Often, when we judge professional competitions, we see dancers who have an opportunity to drive their performance levels higher. If we coach them following the competition, we often have them concentrate on how they too can dance more fully, using tension, tone and torque. While the coaching session might be more detailed and would of course concentrate on more specific and complex details, the basic lesson is still the same.

"Dance your whole body."

This is one of our favorite ideas and we say it all the time.

Think of it like this. You can go on the internet and download the basic step patterns for all the major ballroom dances. In fact, you can go on the internet and download a lesson from us. You can follow the steps. You can practice a little and then you can hold your own on the dance floor. But are you really dancing? You don't want to just walk around in a memorized step pattern, following a video instruction that tells you how to move your feet.

To dance your whole body, you take those steps with your feet and engage the rest of our body... from your feet all the way through the tips of your fingers and the top of your head. You do this through tension, torque and tone. Using the rotation example above, you can easily see how it relates to your smooth dance frame. But it works for rhythm dancing too. The use of tension, torque and tone are what make you absolutely present, in that moment, with your partner.

Chapter Five:
Action Drives the Movement

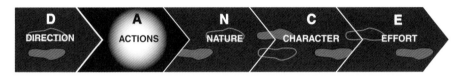

D	A	N	C	E
DIRECTION	ACTIONS	NATURE	CHARACTER	EFFORT

Once you have established direction, the next natural inclination is action. Generations of scientists and artists and physiologists have studied movement and many of them have written and theorized about movement in dance. Once again, our approach is to try to simplify it into a few actionable ideas that will change your perspective on how to think about action in dance.

There are seven actions you should consider for ballroom dancing. All steps can be broken into these seven actions: bending, traveling, twisting, turning, stretching, contracting, and balancing. Remember, our entire philosophy is based on the notion that what you *see* when you watch someone dance is *not* what you *do* when you dance.

Remember this as you think about the specific *action* that drives the *movement*. We hope you find it might be something different than you thought.

27

As an aside, it's worth noting that disagreements occur in all partnerships and ours is no exception. The concept of "balancing" as an action is a place where we disagree quite strongly. Nick believes that balancing is an action because it is a state in which you are controlling energy and momentum, even though you may appear still. Lena believes that an "action" means that there must be movement. So, we have agreed to include it and let you be the judge as to whether it counts as an action. (Lena says she can live with that as long as you "practice, practice, practice.")

To improve both your skill and your artistry, break each ballroom step or movement into the actions it requires. Once you understand the *elements* of each action, you can begin to change how you dance by addressing *each part* of the action individually. Pay attention to what it feels like. Begin to feel the difference, for example, between twisting and turning. Start with your feet. What does it feel like to roll through your foot, or to pivot your foot or to keep it still? How does it feel when you move from one to the other? Are you traveling or are you twisting? Are you bending or are your stretching? Move across the floor and rotate while you are doing it. Are you twisting or turning? Which action is driving your movement?

This is the classic case of what you see – and even how you describe it – is not accurate in describing what you are actually doing. Take an example from the classic ballroom dance, the waltz. In waltz, we say "rise and fall" or "lower" but what we really mean when we say "lower" is that we bend and stretch at the same time. While our knees flex in a "lowering" direction, the top of our spine actually stretches up and doesn't contract at all.

28

One woman we worked with truly believed she would never be able to do a particular turn. When we introduced her to a twisting action and showed her how to twist her body by moving her arms and her torso, the turn was so easy she couldn't believe it. She said, "so I shouldn't be thinking of it as turning? I should be thinking of it as twisting!" Twisting is the preparation for turning; it is the action to create turn. Most important, it is technically what you *do* rather than what you see.

Aha!

Our definitions of The Seven Elements of Action

- **Bending:** to become or make curved or to change or cause to change direction. In dance it is often the flexing of a joint.

- **Traveling:** to go from place to place, or in dance, to transfer your weight from foot to foot.

- **Twisting:** to wind something or make it turn in opposing directions, or in dance, to create torque. (In dance, often the preparation for turning.)

- **Turning:** move to face a different direction or to move around an axis.

- **Stretching:** extend by force or to extend to full length; or in dance, two points moving in opposing directions in a straight line.

- **Contracting:** to shrink or lessen; or tighten or draw together.

- **Balancing:** a state in which two opposing factors are of equal weight or importance so they effectively cancel each other out and stability is maintained, or put simply, getting your weight over your own feet.

Each step contains some or all of these movements. Back to our waltz example: to do a basic box step you must bend (your knee) and stretch (your spine), then you travel, then you stretch and then you contract and begin it again.

Another example is stationary Cuban motion. Start with your weight on your right leg so your left leg is free. To create Cuban motion, bend your free leg (the left one) and stretch from the same side hip to your opposite armpit or side. Your standing leg (the right one) is straight and your side is contracting. Twist the supporting hip back away from the free shoulder. Once you have taken the step, shift to the other leg. We travel to change our weight to the bent leg through a neutral position then repeat the actions, now with the opposite leg and sides… Feel the stretch through your left side. Bend the free leg. Twist through your torso against your hips.

Many of the elements are interrelated; although some lead to each other, they are all separate and distinct. If you are having trouble with a certain part of your dancing, chances are that you are missing or not optimizing an action that is required. For example, you have to contract the muscles before you can stretch. You are constantly moving between these actions - that's dancing! To improve your dancing, break all of this movement into very specific pieces of action and work on them one at a time.

Practice working on each one so you can be much more specific in your "action vocabulary." You need to be able to understand the difference between a twist and a turn, for example, just like you need to know the difference between your lats and your back.

Take a small step. Then take a big step. Then jump.
Experience how each of those feels and how much effort it
takes. Think about the different actions that actually create
the movement.

Try the following to isolate exactly what we mean by each
element. In this chart, we've attempted to help newer
dancers actually translate the concepts into a physical
sensation. While it might seem obvious, try some of the
actions below and concentrate hard on what they feel like in
your body. Focus on the areas we've listed at the right.

To Feel This Element of Action:	Try Doing This:	You Should Focus on Feeling This:
Bend	Touch your toes or sit. Bicep Curl. Squat. Drop your weight, flex your knees, flex your elbows.	The movement of the joint that is flexing (not the muscles).
Travel	Run with big steps, transfer your weight from foot to foot.	The progression of your body from foot to foot.
Twist	Rotate your shoulders against your hips, turn your wrists against your elbows, look over your shoulder as far to the left as you can.	Feel the energy in your muscles as the muscles work against themselves.
Turn	From a torso twist, take a step and rotate your whole body over one foot.	Feel the rotation of the entire "structure" (versus the muscle group).
Stretch	Send your arms straight up to the ceiling; reach out with your arm or leg.	Feel the opposition of the end points of the stretch (push your foot to the ground as your arm goes to the ceiling).
Contract	Curl your body up into a ball, pull your hand in towards your stomach, and put your head on your knees, squeeze an imaginary ball.	Feel the opposite of a stretch – your muscles feel bound and contained in a smaller space, moving inward to a central point.
Balance	Stand on your tiptoes without falling over, lean up against a wall, then push away, hold a doorknob and lean away (but stay on your toes!)	Feel how you can be in control of all the energy within and around your body.

Try these things and think about what they feel like. Once you can isolate what they feel like, try to apply it to some of your ballroom steps.

Try a box step in waltz.

- Turning to the left, you start with your feet (this is true for any left turn).
- Start with your left leg.
- Bend your knees, travel forward (take a step) and start to twist left from hips to shoulders.
- Turn your whole body a 1/4 to the left.
- Stretch you right side, from your toes to your shoulder, as you close your feet.
- Contract back to a neutral position as you start to bend.
- Now repeat the process, this time stepping back with the right foot. (If you were turning to the right you would turn first through your body.)

Think about each of these actions – not just taking the step or lowering, but traveling, twisting, turning and contracting and bending - and try to isolate them. Think carefully about the differences between twisting and turning. They are very different. And think about how they differ from traveling.

Once you start to actually dance, the speed can make you forget about the separate actions since they will all blend together and ultimately feel as one continuous movement. The learning and ability to improve lies in the ability to isolate, separate and practice the various pieces.

Remember, we are talking about actually moving - up or down or side to side. You can certainly do more than one action at a time – in fact you should be. When you "lower" in waltz you are contracting in your legs but you are stretching the muscles around your spine.

Think about a turn you might be struggling with. Chances are you are actually twisting to start the turn too early or travelling in the wrong direction or starting the turn too late. You might be trying to pull your body around with your shoulders instead of twist your hips. You might be trying to torque your body around when you should bend and straighten the knee to get the turn to rotate.

Improving your turn might come from breaking apart what you need to do into its elements and changing how you think about it and how you attack it. One of the most important things you can learn – really learn – is that while you can incorporate different actions into different parts of your body at the same time, you can only move (travel) through space in one direction at a time. The actions flow into each other and often one creates the next, but if you really break it down you will find you are doing different actions but only actually traveling one direction at a time.

Now that you know what the actions are, you need to think about how to dance them in partnership and how to put it to music. The timing of the action to the music and with your partner is the last piece of the physical foundation of the dance. We think of timing in music as the very nature of dance.

Chapter Six:
The Nature of the Ballroom

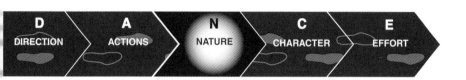

D DIRECTION | A ACTIONS | N NATURE | C CHARACTER | E EFFORT

The Nature of Ballroom Dance

One way we like to think about the very heart of ballroom dancing is that there are not just two parties dancing together on the floor. There are actually three – me, you and "us." I have to dance my part. You have to dance your part. And then we dance together. The elements that connect us into the "we" are these four basic elements of the nature of the ballroom – timing, tempo, breath and connection.

All of us should spend less time looking for the perfect partner and more time being the perfect partner. If we all understand the "natural elements" of the ballroom, we will all be better partners.

Dancing is generally taught by attempting to instruct the physical first and then the musical. We memorize step patterns, turn on the music, count 5-6-7-8 and off we go. You learn one part. Your partner learns the other. Then once you memorize your steps you attempt to do it together.

But are we really dancing? Are we really physically expressing the music?

Consider for a moment how most people look for instructions on how to dance. Do they stand quietly, listening carefully to a piece of music and then thinking about its tempo? No. Instead, they do it this way:

The Traditional Way You Learn A Box Step

1. Look at the diagram in the book
2. Move left foot forward
3. Move right foot to the side
4. Close left foot to right foot
5. Step back with right foot
6. Move left foot to the side
7. Close right foot to left foot

"This is the basic to a waltz which is called a box or a square."

If you follow the set of instructions above, you will have walked a pattern in the shape of a square. We don't want to walk. We want to dance. And, in the ballroom, we want to dance with a partner.

Dancing means we want to experience the most possible impact of a particular action without distorting the form. We want to transform the music from something we hear to something we feel. We want to literally breathe life into the music so it becomes three-dimensional physical movement instead of one-dimensional sound. This is the nature of dance.

As we said, in ballroom dancing – we always do it with a partner. So, as if it were not enough to try to figure out your own role, your own frame, whether you are twisting, traveling or turning, you have to take all of that and connect it with another human being dealing with all the same variables you are. It's exhausting to think about!

So how do you organize all of this? Where do you start?

What determines how you know what your partner will do and what you will do? Go back to the very nature of dance, and specifically ballroom dance: the ideas of music (which is essential to dance) and partnership (which essential to the ballroom).

The dictionary definition of "nature" states that nature is "the forces and processes collectively that control the phenomena of the physical world." Four "natural" ingredients control the physical world of the ballroom. Each dancer interprets and physically manifests *timing, tempo, breath and connection* to turn just plain movement into partner dancing. *Timing* and *tempo* result from the music and provide a road map for the action; *breath* and *connection* are the critical methods of non-verbal communication that are required to dance with a partner.

So let's begin with the music because that's where we get timing and tempo. Music is the natural foundation of dance. It is what makes dance different from other kinds of movement.

"Dancing is the Physical Expression
of the Music Being Played"
~ Neville Boyd O.A.M., J.P.

To dance you must first listen to the music, then really hear the music and then translate the movement back to the music. Every piece of music has a set method of **timing**. You will often hear this referred to as 3-4 or 4-4 time. Those numbers represent how many counts/beats there are in a measure of music of a particular piece.

Tempo is the speed at which the piece moves, and it's measured in beats per minute. Now you understand those two ideas. To understand how it is the "force of nature" in dance, break it back down into pieces. Here's how it works.

Imagine you are listening to a piece of music and you hear timing. This goes something like this: **DA** da da, **DA** da da in even counts. You can feel it: you feel the emphasis on the first beat of the measure (called the downbeat) the one that's emphasized. To decode the timing, count the downbeat as "one" and keep counting until you hear another downbeat.

So you've figured out that you have 3/4 timing – but you could have *fast* 3/4 timing or *slow* 3/4 timing. That's the tempo. The fast tempo would be a Viennese Waltz and the other a Waltz.   As any ballroom beginner knows, these are very difference dances. While they have the same *timing,* the different *tempos* make them feel very different. The same is true for rumba and cha cha. Both are 4/4 time, but they move at different speeds, or different tempos.
Each dancer needs to understand and use the tempo; it's what you need to hear, feel, and translate.

So timing and tempo are the first two governing forces in the ballroom. The secret to translating the music into partnered movement begins with the physical manifestation of that timing. That starts with your *breath*.

Breathing, done correctly, helps hold both you and your partner to the strict tempo and specific timing of each dance. Surprisingly, most dancers rarely give breathing the attention it deserves. A common mistake made by dancers at all levels is that they often hold their breath. In dance, like in yoga or pilates, you cannot do the movement correctly without breathing. Like in weight lifting, breath can give you power, strength and control.

Once you have set yourself up to breathe in time with the music, the last piece left is to remember you're not out there alone. This is, after all, partner dancing, so it is elementary that you must learn how to appropriately *connect* to your partner so that together you can translate the music into your collective movement. Now that you understand the four ingredients, we can get into more detail on each of them.

Drilling Down On Timing and Tempo

In ballroom dancing, tempo is so critical that there are a strict set of rules that set the standards for how fast a piece of music can move to qualify as a certain dance. Be forewarned. Of all the aspects of ballroom dancing, this can feel the most overwhelming. You see all these charts and you think you can't possibly remember it all. But don't worry. The charts that follow are for reference and they may help you clarify the differences between dances or provide a starting point. But don't get hung up on the charts. Use them for reference.

Remember, timing first.

Here is the basic chart of musical timing; it shows the basic timing and tempo of each of the ballroom dances. There are standards in the world of ballroom dancing that define specifically the tempo of each dance. The tempo shown for International and American Style dances are approved (given in Measures per Minute - MPM and Beats per Minute - BPM) as of May, 2009. The chart might seem complicated, it is the best way to understand the differences in tempo between dances.

INTERNATIONAL STYLE DANCES					
	TIMING	PRO/AM **(TEMPO)**		PRO & AMATEUR **(TEMPO)**	
	Beats per Measure	MPM	Beats Per Minute	MPM	Beats Per Minute
BALLROOM					
Waltz	3	28-30	(84-90)	28	(84)
Tango	4	32	(128)	32	(128)
Viennese	3	56-58	(168-174)	56-58	(168-174)
Foxtrot	4	28-30	(112-120)	28-30	(112-120)
Quickstep	4	48-52	(192-208)	48-52	(192-208)
LATIN					
Cha Cha	4	31	(124)	31	(124)
Samba	2	48-50	(96-100)	50	(100)
Rumba	4	27	(108)	26	(104)
Paso Doble	2	60-62	(120-124)	60-62	(120-124)
Jive	4	38-44	(152-176)	44	(176)

Source: National Dance Council of America.
Please visit www.ndca.org for more information.

40

AMERICAN STYLE DANCES					
	TIMING	BRONZE (TEMPO)		ALL OTHERS (TEMPO)	
	Beats per Measure	MPM	Beats Per Minute	MPM	Beats Per Minute
SMOOTH					
Foxtrot	4	32-34	(128-136)	30	(120)
Waltz	3	30-32	(90-96)	28-30	(84-90)
Tango	4	30-32	(120-128)	30	(120)
Peabody	4	60-62	(240-248)	60-62	(240-248)
Viennese	3	54	(162)	54	(162)
RHYTHM					
Bolero	4	24-26	(96-104)	24	(96)
Cha Cha	4	30	(120)	30	(120)
Mambo	4	48-51	(192-204)	47	(188)
Merengue	2	29-32	(58-64)	29-32	(58-64)
Paso Doble	2	58-60	(116-120)	58-60	(116-120)
Rumba	4	32-36	(128-144)	32	(128)
Samba	2	52	(104)	52	(104)
Swing	4	34-36	(136-144)	36	(144)
WC Swing	4	28-32	(112-128)	28-32	(112-128)
Polka	2	60-62	(120-124)	60-62	(120-124)
Hustle	4	28-30	(112-120)	28-30	(112-120)

Source: National Dance Council of America.
Please visit www.ndca.org for more information.

Spend the time you need to listening to various pieces of music and practice recognizing timing and tempo. One good way to practice is to purchase good strict tempo music specifically compiled for the ballroom. It's easy to find CD's and music online that is identified as strict tempo ballroom dance music and labeled on the cover or the insert with not only the type of dance but also the actual tempo. Make a point of connecting what you read on the label with what you hear and you will start to feel more confident.

Listen to lots of music. Find the "1" count - and practice, practice, practice. This is especially important for the leader. Once you have distinguished the downbeat (or the "1" count) you can dance with much more clarity. Yes, the leader has to be great at this since he or she has to start, but it will also help the follower add more clarity to his or her dancing.

Building a basic understanding of music will help you identify what dance it could or should be, help you partner more effectively and help avoid getting into bad habits that could come from timing problems, because, trust us, it's very easy to count wrong.

Many times you hear teachers use different words to count. Some people count in "slows" and "quicks" and some count in numbers. Some people count in measures. Some people talk about phrasing. You will hear a lot of words that are all trying to address timing and tempo. What's important is that you understand and stick to the same system but know that you have options. Some dances are counted in slows and quicks. Some really should be counted numerically. Some dances are counted in numerical sequence.

In ballroom we will quite often count two measures – for example in 4/4 timing we might say 1/2/3/4/5/6/7/8. When counting eight measures, which you might be doing when you are phrasing choreography, teachers often revert to highlighting the downbeat of each measure. For example, 1/2/3/4, 2/2/3/4, 3/2/3/4, 4/2/3/4.

Most of the time, you will hear people refer to "slow" and "quick" unless it's a very quick dance. Quicker dances, like viennese waltz and cha cha, are usually counted in numbers. There is no deep hidden meaning here – it's really for quite a simple reason. When you have to count fast, it works better to stick with the numbers – you can actually say them faster.

Whether you use words or numbers, in the end, though, it doesn't really matter… because what you really need to do is make a sound that represents a beat in a way that is true to the tempo of the music.

Here's an example of how to put it to work for you.

Consider the foxtrot. If you are doing a basic foxtrot you are walking with four steps: forward, forward, side, close. The timing of the dance required that you take the four steps of the pattern to six beats of music. Usually, people count it as "slow, slow, quick, quick." Sometimes this creates a problem and makes it so the basic pattern gets danced in four counts rather than the required six, as the dancer uses each syllable to count as one beat.

To avoid that, try equating the syllables with a beat and replace the word "slow" with "slowly" which then makes it easy to take the first step on 1-2, the second on 3-4 and the side step on 5 and then the close on the 6. So now you have six syllables - one for each best of music: "slow-ly, slow-ly, quick quick."

Expanding on this idea, here is a suggestion for some other dances. Sometimes we use, three quarter, half and quarter beats in a measure of music. Here's how you can accommodate that. Say these words out loud while you are learning and practicing:

- For one whole beat say the word "whole"
- For a half beat say the word "and" or say the word "half"
- For a quarter beat say the word "a"
- Counting by numbers will also help, depending on the dance, particularly for a 6 or 8 count dance…1,2,3,4,5, 6, 7, 8. This works best for single count dances like merengue or single swing, dances with straight timing

Now, let's put it all together. Go back to the example earlier where you download the instructions for a basic step pattern. This time, you've learned the basic American foxtrot step pattern. And you've just learned how to count the tempo. You understand the concepts of timing and tempo in the music. Now you have to put the two together and actually move to the music.

No matter what level dancer you are, timing and tempo are critical to success in the ballroom, not only because they are the way you connect to the music but also because they serve as the backbone upon which you build your partnership.

Breath

Every ballroom dancer has or will have the chance to see more experienced dancers at work. You might be surprised to see how they practice. Often you can't hear any music and yet they move together. Often they are practicing in a studio that is playing music totally different from the dance they are practicing. You know they are doing a mambo and yet you hear a waltz. How are they able to do that, not just on their own but how are they able to both hear the same music that isn't playing?

If you watch closely, you might hear the less experienced dancers actually counting out loud. The next level up might be mouthing "slow" and "quick" (or if we'd been in town lately, "slowly" and "quick"). But quite often you don't see professionals appear to be counting at all. We can go out on the dance floor with no music, without talking to each other, and we can both start to waltz in perfect time with each other.

How do we do it?

First, we establish a pattern through when and how we breathe and our bodies follow the motion. We can sense it in each other. Even the newest dancer can easily follow a highly skilled leader. It's not just that they send you firmly in the right direction (more on that in a minute) but they also send you conscious, non-verbal signals by how they breathe.

Learn to breathe on the correct beats (the timing) and you can then learn the speed at which you will take those breaths (the tempo).

We often discover that breathing in dancing is a concept that is overlooked by most dance curricula until well after you've taken many lessons or classes and sometimes, it isn't touched on until you are a highly competitive dancer. While it is difficult to explain what "breathing in time" means until you have danced the dance and done it with a partner, we encourage people to at least think about the basic concepts of breathing much earlier in their dancing learning. In fact, we like to teach it from the very beginning.

Breathing correctly, and working to perfect how you breathe, will save you great amounts of effort, focus and energy later on. Here are three concepts to think about when it comes to the basics of breathing.

First, as you've already guessed, *your breath patterns in ballroom are a reflection of the timing and tempo of the music*. There are variations, later on, but think of a waltz. The 3/4 time of it is very clear. When you do waltz, we think breathing is as important as rise and fall.

Second, like yoga, pilates or martial arts, *used correctly, your breath can give you power and create energy*. When you are in the gym, you expel your breath to create the effort it takes to lift the weight. This is no different when you are dancing.

Third, *breathing connects you with your partner* and helps make the sum of the parts greater than the individual. Breathing together will make you more connected, it will help you lead and follow and it will help you move together instead of feeling you are sometimes at odds with your partner. In short, breathing is the first step in creating the "us."

Here are some basic breathing patterns for some of the ballroom dances. As you get more experienced, or you start working on more complex choreography, this can change, but here are some basic guidelines. You may note that generally the breathing patterns are in sync with the amount of energy you are expending in each measure. Some people might have a different breathing pattern for some of these dances. And, of course, there are more dances. Try it for yourself and see what feels right to you. The main thing is that you and your partner establish the pattern and you breathe in sync with each other and the music.

This chart shows our breathing patterns (another example of trying to forge a partnership where you don't always agree...). Think about yours and use the chart to record them.

Dance	Timing	Breathe In	Breathe Out	Your Breathing
Waltz V. Waltz	3/4	5,6	1,2,3,4	
Foxtrot	4/4	7,8	1,2,3,4/5,6	
Tango	4/4	7,8	1,2,3,4,5,6	
Viennese Waltz	3/4	5,6	1,2,3,4	
Quickstep	4/4	7,8	1,2,3,4,5,6	
Rumba	4/4	8,1	2,3,4/5,6,7	
Cha Cha	4/4	4,1,2,3	4,1,2,3	
Mambo	4/4	7,8,1	2,3,4,5,6	
Swing	4/4	7,8	1,2,3,4,5,6	
Bolero	4/4	8,1,2	3,4,5,6,7	
Merengue	4/4	7,8	1,2,3,4,5,6	
Hustle	4/4	&1	2,3,4,5,6,7,8	
West Coast Swing*	4/4	5,6	1,2,3,4	
Paso Doble	2/4	7,8	1,2,3,4,5,6	

breathing listed in chart for six-count West Coast; for eight-count, breathe in on 7,8

With the timing, tempo and breathing established, you can – finally – connect to your partner and feel you are starting to dance together.

Connection

Connection – which is the communication and transference of information, both within your own body and with your partner – is one of the most challenging concepts in ballroom to write about. It's difficult since it is, by definition, non-verbal. In ballroom dancing, connection is

48

accomplished through the principles we've outlined here – working together on the same timing, tempo and breath patterns. ("Nick," says Lena, "why do you insist on finding words to describe something you can only feel?")

In the context of this book there are a few key ideas to think about and practice as it relates to connection.

First, timing and tempo help govern connection. Hearing the patterns in the music, adopting them in your breathing patterns and working on the same tempo as your partner give you the map you need to ultimately arrive at your shared destination at the same time.

Two Types of Connection

It's important to understand that there are two kinds of connection. The first is a physical connection. It is experienced through touch and feel of various parts of your and your partner's bodies. The other is visual connection. It is, quite literally, sight. Both are equally powerful and good dancing is not possible without both. When you watch couples out on the floor, you will notice that the ones who are actively aware of each other and are paying visual attention to each other are more connected and more as one.

Connect With Yourself and Then With Your Partner

A most important aspect of connection – and one you might not have considered – is your own internal connection. Your internal connection is how you create the tone in your body that allows you to receive and transfer messages of direction and intent through time and space. If you are really connected to yourself, the following will be evident:

1. You are ready for action, with the appropriate amount of tone in your body
2. You are in control of your own energy
3. You are visually connected to your partner
4. You feel harmonious physical connection with your partner

Once again, what a spectator sees and what a dancer does to achieve what you want to display are quite different. In this case, to connect, you actually have to create resistance. If you have the appropriate level of resistance – read: tone – the leader will be able to signal direction and the follower will be able to react. Then you can move in any direction together. This is not quite as sloppy or physical as it sounds. When both dancers share the nonverbal connection we've outlined, one dancer signals and the other responds through, yes, pushing and pulling.

Chapter Seven:
Determine Your Character

D	A	N	C	E
DIRECTION	ACTIONS	NATURE	CHARACTER	EFFORT

Now that you have established your direction, the actions you will use to get there, and the forces of nature in the ballroom you can put to work, you need to move to the next level and start applying your own judgment, artistry and style. This begins with character and will be carried on in the section of *effort*.

All dance is made up of characterization and the movement that expresses that character. We like to think of the character as the "life force" of the dance. It's the one element that comes from the music that you bring to life. It's a force that is not just physical; it is bigger than the individual. This is why it is so important to understand and channel.

Character is the quality that makes each dance unique and essentially serves as the "destination" for each dancer. Even to the untrained observer, you can feel it when a dancer truly gets the character of the dance and adapts it into his or her own style.

51

Each dance is like a story and each story has a character and a personality which you must know before you begin. Once you know the character, you begin the movement that creates the character. Each dance differs in its execution or performance because we put an individual style upon it. We can dance a tango and it can feel very different from the tango you see in the local studio. It's not because ours is on national television – it's because everyone will express himself or herself in a different way.

Both can be great but both will probably be very different. What the performances will share, though, is the sense of drama and passion that is the tango. Done "right" (the extent that there is a '"right" way) you may not know the step and you might be surprised by the style, but you will recognize the character of your old friend, the tango. How you move is really what dance is all about but you can't possibly decide how to move unless you are clear on the character you are trying to achieve.

Finding the Character

As you consider each dance, consider what is at its heart. Think about how it looks and feels and the mood you want to create when you dance it. Describing the character of the dance does not have to be complicated. In fact, we prefer a simple and helpful trick - think of just one word to describe it. It's funny how easy this is to do and how, if pressed, most dancers can come up with a word. Often, though, even professional dancers don't use this method as a starting point. We do, and while we sometimes disagree on the word, we definitely agree on the method. Try to use this as a framework for discovering the character of each dance.

Think about how you feel when you do it, when you watch it, when you hear the music. Sometimes, you may experience

three different characters. When you do, watch or listen!
Think about the single thing that best captures the essence
of the dance for you. However you get there – by watching,
listening, feeling, thinking - choose that one word.

Here are our words, the ones we think about when we think
about choreographing, dancing or judging a competition.
Think about each of the dances. Which word would you
use? Remember, you're looking for a word that is meaningful
and inspiring to YOU – what drives you and helps you feel
the character of the dance. We encourage you to literally fill
out this list and remember your word each time you begin
your practice or your performance or even your social
dancing.

Dance	Nick Says	Lena Says	You Say
Waltz	Elegance	**Soft**	
International Foxtrot	Sophisticated	**Playful**	
American Foxtrot	Jazzy	**Flirty**	
Tango	Passionate	**Dramatic**	
International Viennese Waltz	Stately	**Classic**	
American V. Waltz	Balletic	**Romantic**	
Quickstep	Light	**Happy**	
American Rumba	Sexy	**Playful**	
Cha Cha	Fun	**Cheeky**	
Mambo	Earthy	**Rhythmical**	
Swing	Cool	**Swingy**	
Bolero	Romantic	**Sexy**	
Jive	Bouncy	**Jumpy**	
Paso Doble	Arrogant	**Fight**	
International Rumba	**Lustful**	**Passionate**	

One More Thought

A famous New Zealander, John Delroy, once suggested a wonderful way to think about the character of the dance was to study different kinds of animals and watch how they move.

Then he asked you to compare their movements to a specific dance. For example: consider the tango and think about the movements of a panther. Another way to think about the character of a dance is to think about actors. For the foxtrot, perhaps Ginger Rogers comes to mind. Another way to think about it is to consider movement of natural or manmade objects to describe dances. Does the thought of a Ferrari remind you of the quickstep? What dance do you think of when you see a tree swaying in the wind? Write down and use some of them and see if they help you define the character.

Remember your dance keyword! Come back to it every so often and see if you still like it. Feel free to let it evolve. Feel free to change it. But definitely use it. Once you have established the character, you have your destination. How you reach your destination is through movement.

Chapter Eight:

Effort Drives the Action

D	A	N	C	E
DIRECTION	ACTIONS	NATURE	CHARACTER	EFFORT

Before you read further, please answer the following questions....

1. Do you think of dancing as "heavy" or "light?"

2. Which word best describes the following dances?

Waltz	☐ Heavy	☐ Light
Tango	☐ Heavy	☐ Light
Foxtrot	☐ Heavy	☐ Light

I've asked these questions to thousands of dancers in ballrooms around the world and almost every time, people are surprised when I tell them my answer to these questions. I hope the answers surprise you, but I also hope once you review the ideas of "effort" in your dancing, you will find that your answers might be similar to mine.

You create action through effort. "Effort" is the key. We don't mean effort as in "trying" or "I'm making an effort" – we mean effort as in the physical dimensions that create the action. Done right, it should actually make your dancing appear effortless! Remember at the beginning we said this would take time and practice. Well, it takes something else too.

It Takes Patience

This method is not something you can read and then do immediately. Sure, you can begin to apply it immediately and you can begin to think in this way immediately but you really have to practice it. This approach outlines a number of different concepts that can apply to every variety of ballroom dancing, so there is a lot to think about it. You can't possibly think of all that we will share all at once, but you can take advantage of the fact that dancing is still based upon a condition reflex action... you can do it repetitively to build into your muscle memory. It will take time and practice.

The key to harnessing effort is to understand the overall approach and then to break it into pieces and apply it, one piece at a time. You have to do it over and over and over again. But the outcome will be worth it. You will feel better about your dancing; you will deepen your understanding of what it takes to change the way you dance

What's the Order?

The next question most people ask is, "OK, I know I have to break it into pieces but after that what order should I work on these things?" The answer is that you can go in any order you want. You can choose the dance that you feel comes most naturally, that you have the most comfort with or that you feel you learn best in.

There really is no one way – or order –to teach and practice these concepts. But it is important the break things down into the most basic pieces. For each action, there are four dimensions that lead to how it appears when you dance it. If you consider each dimension as you are learning the dance, it will help power the muscle memory you are developing.

"WEST" - The Four Dimensions of Effort

Each action is made up of effort and each effort has four dimensions. Effort can be broken into four dimensions. Each dimension must be a choice between two extremes:

- Weight
- Energy
- Space
- Time

For each action in each dance, we use the dimensions of effort that flow from the character of that dance. It's a lot to think about, so break it into pieces and work on it one at a time.

Weight is Heavy or Light

The first aspect is *weight:* how we move our weight, how we shift our weight and how we portray the use of our weight. Weight is one of two extremes, depending on the dance: a dance is heavy or a dance is light. We can use our physical body weight to show heaviness or lightness.

Most of the major dances require that we incorporate the "heavy" aspect of weight. The physical manifestation of "heavy" in dance is generally considered that everything is working downwards. Many people describe it as if the floor were magnetic and the soles of your shoes were metal, that you need to push your feet into the floor and feel the downward pressure. And, no surprise, when you think of the effort of "light" you can think of it as the opposite... that everything is going up.

To illustrate the concept of "heavy," think of lifting heavy suitcases, or think about leaning over to pick up a barbell. To illustrate the concept of light, think about a bird the moment it lifts off the ground.

Weight and how you use it combine with the other aspects of effort to ultimately create the action that drives the movement. Think about weight as the starting point and it will give you a clear and simple focus.

Energy Is Bound or Free

The second dimension is *energy:* how we capture our energy, how we expel it and how we portray energy in the way we dance. The two extremes in the energy dimension are whether the energy is "bound" or "free."

An easy way to think about bound energy is to think of squeezing a ball in your fist. It feels strong and controlled. Or, think of picking up a brick. Slowly raise it in front of you with your arm outstretched. To illustrate "free" energy, swing your arm. Feel how it goes in a direction until something sends it back. Send it back, as freely as it went, but do so intentionally.

Space is Direct or Flexible

The third dimension is *space:* space can be "direct" or "flexible." This dimension describes the relationship of your body moving through space. It does not mean the direction or line you are traveling, but the motion of your body as it makes an action. You can have flexible effort while traveling

59

on a straight line. Direct feels more sharp and severe. Flexible is more fluid and continuous. Direct space is more cubic or rectangular. Flexible – as it relates to the space dimension - is more of a curve.

Try hanging your arm straight down past your hip. Lift it straight out to the side. That is direct in the dimension of space. Put your arm back down by your side and lift it to the same ending position, but lift up your elbow first and then your wrist. Point your fingers out. You will end up in the same position but you will have used space in a way that is "flexible" and not direct.

Time is Sudden or Sustained

The final fourth aspect is *time*. Think of it first as an amount of time, or how long it takes to change movement or direction, and how long it then takes to get from Point A to Point B. The two extremes of the time dimension in dance are whether the effort is sudden or sustained or, said another way, quick and slow.

These two extremes address the pace at which you release or capture energy. Your ability to control time and your movement within it is based on how you can physically contain or control energy – energy that comes from momentum, or the resistance against momentum, energy you can use to create drive or slow it down.

Consider this. Gravity is pulling us down at a rate of over 32 feet per second. That means that when you are up in the air, balanced on your toes, rather than lowering –which you would naturally do so fast that you wouldn't ever be up – you are actually fighting the force of gravity. Time – or timing – is something you can control by physically resisting the forces of gravity. You have the ability to slow it down or speed it up.

60

Any movement from A to B can be done on a quick or a slow. The greater the distance the longer it takes. That means, more effort if you want to cover that distance in a shorter amount of time.

If you were moving from point A to Point B, you could move there on a slow, or you could move there on a quick and get there twice as fast. You still get to the same place but think how different it feels, and how different the effort is in doing it quickly or slowly.

The energy you put into it is relative to how fast you want to move. For example, if you want to get there on a quick, you have to move twice as fast – which requires twice the energy – as a you would to get to the same spot on a slow.

This one is so obvious that a lot of people miss it. How quick can you make it? How slow can you make it? How much can you make it sudden or how much can you sustain it?

Both require focus on *bound energy*. For example, consider an underarm turn in rumba. You might slow down the first movement by sustaining it. And then you might want to do more sudden timing as you flip around in the actual turn. Then you would slow it down as you move apart and then make it sudden again as you come back together. This is one of the best ways to add style and spice to your dancing.

Dancing is not about the beats – it's about understanding the timing and the beats and then about filling the space in between the beats with movement. Once you start working on the efforts it is a personal decision that you make as to what you want it to be.

Putting It All Together

We use the acronym WEST to describe these dimensions of effort. The more you think about it and the more you practice, the more you will be able to connect the dimensions of effort with the character of the dance. When you combine the correct effort you will create stronger, more definitive actions. You will do a better job of achieving the appropriate character for each dance.

Think of the combination in this way. Imagine yourself as an archer. Stretch up and stand tall and imagine you are holding a bow and arrow. Lift both arms up. Bend your body so you can bend your elbow back. The action you take is stretching and bending. The effort that goes in can completely change how the action looks. Make your weight heavy, your energy bound, your space direct and your time sustained. You will be a powerful warrior archer. If you switch the effort on all four dimensions, you can see an archer who looks more like a floppy clown than a powerful warrior. And, since the character of the archer is one of pride and strength, you will see very clearly how the effort comes together appropriate to the character.

"W-E-S-T" and the Major Dances

For each of the major dances, the character of it is created through actions that combine one aspect of each dimension. This chart outlines the various combinations that are used in each dance. Everything you need to know about ballroom dancing... all in one place!

DANCE	WEIGHT	ENERGY	SPACE	TIMING	CHARACTER
	Heavy or Light	Bound or Free	Direct or Flexible	Sudden or Sustained	
Waltz	Heavy	Bound	Direct	Sustained	Elegance **Soft**
American Foxtrot	Heavy-ish	Free	Flexible	Sustained	Sophisticated **Romantic**
International Foxtrot Tango	Light	Bound	Direct	Sudden	Passionate **Dramatic**
Viennese Waltz	Heavy	Bound	Direct	Sudden	Stately **Moving**
Quickstep	Light	Free	Direct	Sudden	**Light Happy**
American Rumba	Heavy	Bound	Flexible	Sustained	Sexy **Playful**
Cha Cha	Light	Free	Direct	Sudden	Fun **Cheeky**
Mambo	Heavy	Free	Flexible	Sudden	Earthy **Rhythmical**
Swing	Heavy	Bound	Direct	Sustained	Cool **Swingy**
Bolero	Heavy	Free	Direct	Sustained	Romantic **Sexy**

Clearly, each of these dimensions in each dance could be an entire chapter by itself. The idea, though, is to start to incorporate them into your dancing and compare them from dance to dance. The awareness you create in your mind will begin to translate into the movement you create through your body.

Chapter Nine:
Take the First Step. Again.

And so there you have it. Our "simple" formula.

The joy and frustration of dance can be captured in how there is enough in each basic concept to last a lifetime. It's hard to decide if you want to work on one or many pieces of a step or a dance, concentrate on a specific dance or focus on a particular style. But wherever you choose to start, we encourage you to start. You may not plunge in like a fearless child but there is most certainly a lesson about starting without barriers that we can take from fearless children.

The mystery of dance is that nothing is as it appears.

The beauty of dance is that once you, the dancer, learn this, you can begin to evolve your dancing. It doesn't matter which aspect you work on first. However, it is helpful to work on one thing and then work on something related – either a different part of the same dance or a different dance with the same subject. For example, think about the character in each of the dances you do and practice those. Or take a cha cha and work on the weight, energy, space and time efforts.

Even if you simply understand the concepts outlined in our **DANCE** formula, you will be a better dancer. Remember, here is what we covered.

D DIRECTION	A ACTIONS	N NATURE	C CHARACTER	E EFFORT
Leading	Bending	Timing	Waltz	Weight
Following	Traveling	Tempo	Tango	Energy
Individual Roles	Twisting	Breath	Foxtrot	Space
Structure	Turning	Connection	Viennese Waltz	Time
Tension	Contracting		Quickstep	
Tone	Stretching		Rumba	
Torque	Balancing		Cha Cha	
			Swing	
			Mambo	
			Jive	
			Balero	

© 2012 Nikoz International

65

It begins with you, the individual and the direction you set: your tone, your frame and the clarity with which you see your job. You are responsible for your part whether you are leading or following. Neither is more important than the other because one cannot exist in the ballroom without the other. Once you have that, you begin to flow to your partner – your breathing, your connection and your shared sense of the character of the dance. Throughout your dancing life, you can always improve your movement. You can always understand your action and work on the elements of your effort.

The two parts of ballroom dancing are not, in the end, the leading and the following, They are the individual and the partnership. They are inseparable and inextricable within each person and within the couple. And yet, to get better, you have to take them apart, understand what they are, and work on getting better individually and then better together.

Chapter Ten:
Effort Never Ends

As we were working on this book we were taking a break from writing and sitting at our favorite Greek restaurant in Los Angeles.

The night air was cool; the owner of the restaurant was happily updating us on what happened on the most recent episode of ABC's "Dancing With the Stars." The tables around us were filled with people enjoying a meal with their friends and family. The sounds of soft music, the flourish of clinking glasses, and the softness of the evening lights surrounded us.

We were talking about all the various things we were doing – creating ideas for new dresses and suits, reviewing a packing list for the professional show we were doing that weekend and how we had to leave at five in the morning.... thinking about the upcoming travel schedule that had us going from coast to coast and back again.... These are nice problems to have but, for a moment, we felt a bit overwhelmed.

For a while there was silence. We'd been talking about what dancing can do for people most of the day. Lena looked up, clearly a little tired, and said, "it's too bad we don't have dancing as a hobby." Nick thought about it for a minute and said, "but we get to dance all the time."

Lena smiled, a little sadly. She paused. Then she said that wasn't what she meant. "It's our profession," she explained.

After another moment, Lena said, "I would love to have taken lessons with you when I was learning." Nick smiled, a little wistfully, and thought about it. And then he said, "we still have a lot to learn."

There was a long silence. Greek music filled the soft night air. Laughter covered the sound of someone dropping a wine glass. Time was suspended for just a moment as we both thought about learning to dance.

Lena looked up and smiled again and said, "Well, we could go learn Argentine tango." Her eyes sparkled.

Silence. And we thought about it. We both thought about how we could learn something together.... we could learn to dance all over again.... we can always get better...

And in that moment all was right with the world.

Life is, after all, a great glorious dance.

About the Authors

Nick and Elena Bacheva Kosovich have danced together for twelve years. Lena is originally from Siberia, Russia, and started dancing at the age of five. Nick hails from Perth, Western Australia, and has been dancing since he was 9 years old. They have lived in the United States for twenty years.

Together, they are World American Ballroom Champions, United States American Ballroom Champions, United States National Classic Showdance Champions, World Classic Showdance runners-up, and two-time World Ten-Dance semi-finalists.

They hold more than 40 professional Showdance and American Ballroom titles including Nevada Star Ball, Embassy Ballroom Championships. American Star Ball, Heritage, Triple Crown, Florida State Championships, Manhattan Dancesport Championships, Millennium, Emerald Ball, Empire State, Unique, World Dance-o-Rama, and New York Dance-o-Rama Open Professional Smooth Champions.

Together, they represented either the United States or Australia to nine separate world championships and for three years they were Arthur Murray National Smooth Champions. They are Former Australian Ten-Dance Representatives and Australian Open Grand Finalists in Latin and Standard.

In addition to their spectacular professional competitive dance career, Nick and Lena have appeared together and separately in numerous television productions and films and are sought-after choreographers and costume designers. In 2010, Nick served as head judge for the US at the 2010 Secundo Campeonato De Baille-Bailando Por Un Sueno in Mexico City; they were principal dancers for the televised "2008 Academy Awards." Costume designers for the inaugural season, they also choreographed the semi-final and final show for Oxygen Cable TV's "Dance Your Ass Off." Nick and Lena have been professional dancers for ABC's "Dancing with the Stars" and have choreographed or coached every season of the #1 show in America, including coaching four the mirror-ball championship winners. They've appeared on Good Morning America, the Ellen Degeneres Show, Soap Talk, E Entertainment News Extra and TV Guide. Nick has appeared in numerous films including "Shall We Dance" (principal dancer), "Everybody Says I Love You" (principal dancer), "Blue in the Face" (Principal Dancer), "Mango Tango" (Actor/ Principal Dancer) and "Only with You" (Actor/ Principal Dancer).

Sought after as judges and coaches around the world, Nick and Lena are among some of the most well-known and well-respected ballroom dancers in the world.

Through their design and style company, LeNique, Nick and Lena design and make elegant, custom-design clothing for ladies and gentlemen. Their creations have been seen on world stages from Olympic figure skating to most major television networks ("So You Think You Can Dance" on Fox, ABC's "Dancing With the Stars," and "Dance Your Ass Off" on Oxygen.)

Their commitment to teaching and passion for the power of ballroom dance can be seen in every aspect of their lives. When they are not coaching, they are teaching. When they are not teaching they are judging ballroom competitions. When they are not judging, they are choreographing. When they are not choreographing, they are thinking up new ways to share their passion for the artistry and power of dance through costume design, new entertainment content and new ways to inspire others to become even better dancers.